ROBERT MAASS

A
is
for
Autumn

SCHOLASTIC INC.
New York Toronto London Auckland
Sydney Mexico City New Delhi Hong Kong

A

is

for

Autumn

and

Apples,

of

course.

B

is

for

Birds

that

fly

south

to

warmer

winter

homes.

C

is

for

Colors

as

leaves

begin

to

change.

D

is

for

Daylight,

getting

shorter

as

the

weather

gets

colder.

E

is

for

Exercise.

You

can

never

get

too

much

of

it.

F

is

for

Frost,

when

dew

freezes

and

water

turns

to

ice.

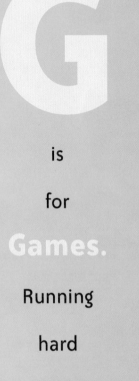

G

is

for

Games.

Running

hard

keeps

away

the

chills.

H

is

for

Halloween.

Bring

out

the

spooky

costumes!

I

is

for

Ice

Cream,

which

is

delicious

in

any

season.

J

is

for

Jacket.

It's

getting

chilly!

K

is

for

Kayak,

taking

one

last

paddle

for

the

season.

L

is

for

Leaves

littering

the

ground

with

vibrant

color.

M

is

for

Monarch

butterfly

gathering

nectar

before

the

long

migration

home.

N

is

for

Neighborhood.

It's

where

we

live.

O

is

for

Owl,

a

bird

of

the

night.

P

is

for

Pumpkins.

They

come

in

lots

of

shapes

and

colors.

Q

is

for

Quilt,

for

that

extra

layer

of

warmth.

R

is

for

Rake.

Time

to

gather

fallen

leaves

before

snow

comes.

S

is

for

Scarecrow

stuffed

with

corn

husks

and

standing

tall.

T

is

for

Thanksgiving

when

families

and

friends

share

a

special

meal.

U

is

for

Umbrella,

keeping

us

dry

in

the

cool

autumn

rain.

V

is

for

Vegetables

like

gourds

and

squash.

W

is

for

Wood

burning

in

fireplaces

to

keep

us

warm.

X

is

for

**Train
Crossing,**

letting

us

know

when

trains

are

near.

Y

is

for

Yellow

as

bright

as

afternoon

sunshine.

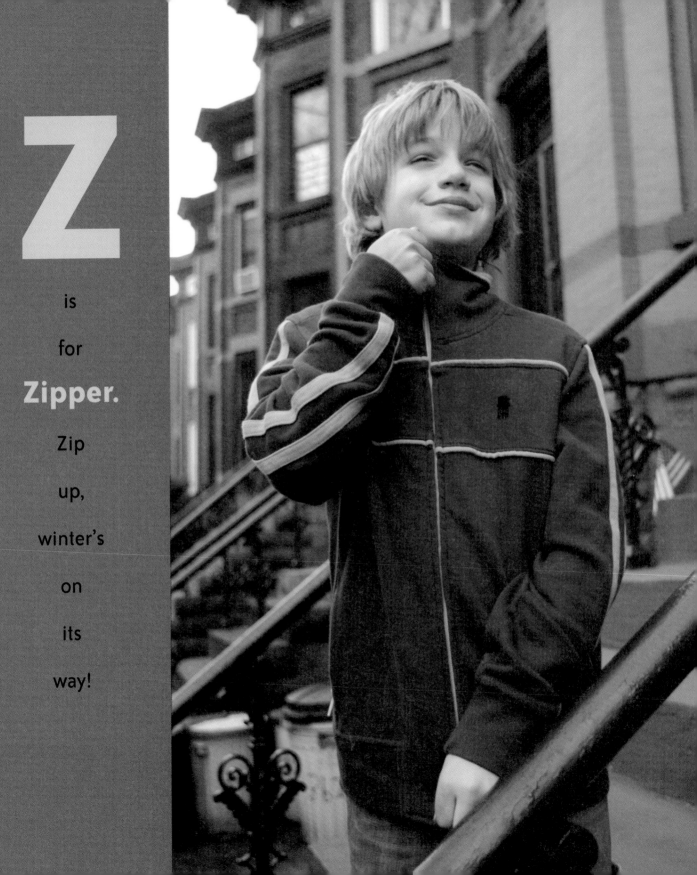

Z

is

for

Zipper.

Zip

up,

winter's

on

its

way!

ISBN 978-0-545-48095-6

Copyright © 2011 by Robert Maass.
All rights reserved. Published by Scholastic Inc.,
557 Broadway, New York, NY 10012, by arrangement
with Henry Holt and Company, LLC. SCHOLASTIC and
associated logos are trademarks and/or registered
trademarks of Scholastic Inc.

12 11 10 9 8 7 6   13 14 15 16 17/0

Printed in the U.S.A.   40

First Scholastic printing, September 2012

Designed by April Ward